What About Me?

An irreverent guide to keeping your marbles when someone you love struggles with mental illness

Ran Weingartner

Weingartner Books

Copyright © 2023 by Ran Weingartner

All rights reserved.

No portion of this book may be reproduced in any form without written permission from the publisher or author, except as permitted by Canadian and U.S. copyright law.

Acknowledgments

It takes a village to get through life. It also takes a village to write a book.

This book wouldn't be possible without the mentorship, the patience, the knowledge, the wisdom and the friendship of the following people. I could write a whole book about what you mean to me.

In no particular order:

My therapist Brenda Quenneville MSW, RP who inspired many of these chapters.

My editor JP Rindfleisch IX, J Thorn and The Author Life Community.

My dad and meticulous line editor and proofreader Erich Weingartner. I wouldn't be half the writer I am without your mentorship over the years.

My friends and psychotherapists Mike Hughes and Brooke Bertrand who read this book and lended their expertise in Borderline Personality Disorder and relationship dynamics.

The love of my life, Molly, and our dog Charlie.

For Molly.

Contents

Chapter 1

What Kind of Book Is This Anyway?

Many books have been written by professionals for professionals about mental illness.

This isn't one of them.

Many more books have been published about how to care for people who are elderly, sick or disabled in some way.

This isn't one of those either.

This book is what I learned about staying sane while my wife's brain periodically tries to kill her.

I am not a therapist, psychiatrist or professional healthcare worker. I am an admin professional by day and a writer by night. I am a recovering addict who periodically needs her meds adjusted.

I'm also a queer woman (in both senses of the word) and the love of my life struggles with Borderline Personality Disorder and Bipolar II.

I swear - suddenly and unexpectedly - and blow off steam with sarcasm.

In other words, my only credentials for writing this book are that my wife - my beautiful, creative, loving wife - is afflicted with mental illness.

And this book is the book I wish I had found when I thought I was losing my mind with stress, fear and despair.

Chapter 2
My Story

Molly and I met at a yoga meditation class in our one-gas-station town. Our first date was at a Chinese food restaurant in a strip mall. We were pretty impressed to have found each other - the only two lesbians within a million-mile radius.

We weren't, but that's what it felt like at the time.

We talked about what brought us back to the area after a lifetime away. She poked at a slippery cashew with her chopsticks.

"I have Borderline Personality Disorder. I know I put my ex through a lot."

I glanced at her over my glasses. Having survived a previous relationship with a person suffering from BPD, I thought I knew all about it.

"Are you sure they got it right? My ex had BPD and they wouldn't own up to anything. Just the fact that you *say* you have BPD probably means you don't. Are you gonna eat that?"

She pushed the plate in my direction, saying nothing. I didn't know it at the time, but I was perpetuating the stigma of mental illness in general, and Borderline Personality Disorder in particular.

Over the months, though, I began to see it. There was a pattern to it. Molly would fixate on a perceived slight for days. She would develop headaches. She would take time off work. She would become irritable, misread situations, and get unreasonably angry.

Eventually, she would stop sleeping. Soon after that, the bottom would fall out.

She'd stay in bed for days, playing video games. Going out became an ordeal. It would take days to recover from a simple grocery run. The lights were too bright. Sound was grating to her. Touch made her skin burn.

No stranger to depression, I didn't immediately freak out. I recognized the signs. I knew what worked for me: call the doctor; get my meds tweaked; go to therapy; start meditating again; hang on for dear life until things lift.

She must be doing something wrong, I thought

Coming home from work, I would find her still in bed. Only our dog Charlie was in a different position than when I had left.

"Are you taking your meds?"

"Yes."

"Are you taking them in the morning?"

Irritated silence.

"Are you hungry?"

"No, thank you."

"Want to come for a walk with Charlie and me?"

"No, thank you."

Heaving an audible sigh, I would collapse into the sofa not knowing what to do with myself.

What was happening?

I cajoled, I nagged, I lectured her about following my roadmap, absolutely convinced it would work for her as it does for me.

It didn't.

Medication regimens came and went. They either had no effect at all or made things worse.

I took over the household chores: the cooking, the cleaning, the groceries, the feeding and walking Charlie. I got up and went to work every day. I drove her to appointments and picked up meds from the drugstore.

Our savings evaporated. I sat helplessly as she pleaded with social service authorities to be placed on disability to supplement our income. I helped her fill out forms. And more forms. And more forms.

Mental illness is a hard sell. You're faking until you prove otherwise. Many illnesses aren't considered debilitating enough. Worse, some are not considered illnesses at all, but a deficiency of moral character.

She'll get better, I told myself. She'll come back to me. We'll dust off our dreams and plans from the mantle, and I'll get my happily ever after. I just had to wait for the professionals to get her on the right cocktail of meds.

I was right.

Sort of.

Molly did get better, and I saw my Happily Ever After rising like the morning sun.

But it didn't last. The headaches returned, followed by the insomnia, the crippling anxiety, and finally a soul-crushing depression. Once again, it all came to a grinding halt.

The same cycle repeated itself every few months.

In the good months, I was amazed by Molly's creativity and productive energy. Every endeavor she started was met with success. At one time, she started an art business and soon had acquired months' worth of commissions to produce. Another time, she started a doggie daycare in our neighborhood, filled to capacity within three months.

But eventually, every effort became too much. The same pattern repeated itself: stress, headaches, insomnia, anxiety, depression, close shop.

I once confided this pattern to a friend, who burst out laughing, "Oh my god, I don't know how you do it. If it were me, I'd have left a long time ago."

I wasn't sure how I was doing it, but leaving Molly was the last thing on my mind.

I knew she meant to make me feel better: I was a survivor! I had grit! I was loyal.

But it didn't make me feel better. It made me feel defensive.

She was my warrior, my wounded Fisher Queen. And I was her Knight of the Round Table.

Actually, I was more like the kitchen maid that peeled potatoes,and emptied piss pots while the knights sat at the round table pondering their next quest. But the point is... I wasn't going anywhere.

I also didn't know how much longer I could keep up this pace. I felt as though I would burst at the seams. I was furious, but I could see how hard she was trying to get better. I could see with my own eyes the effort she was putting into her recovery. She wasn't doing this *to me*.

By the time I got home that evening, my head exploded. I burst into a sobbing rage. I drew a bath to try to calm my nerves. It wasn't working. I couldn't stop sobbing.

Molly sat on the bathroom floor, determined not to leave my side. "I'm sorry," she whispered. "I'm so sorry."

"It's not your fault!" I shouted. "I'm just so mad and I don't know what to do about it!"

I didn't know where to direct this rage and disappointment. Except inward.

I wasn't trying hard enough to keep it together, I told myself. I should be grateful - others have it worse. I was scared. I felt like I had been running but was only barely managing not to fall behind. My whole life had been taken over by work and chores and watching the life drain from the woman I love.

I needed help.

I didn't need someone to tell me it was okay to leave her.

I didn't need someone to tell me I was a saint for sticking it out.

I didn't need someone to tell me to take a bubble bath.

And I definitely didn't need someone to tell me it was her fault, that she was taking advantage of me, that she was a slacker.

What I needed was to know I was not alone. That what we were going through is not uncommon, is natural, is surmountable.

What I needed was someone to show me how to keep from becoming Molly's nursemaid, parent or life coach. I needed someone to tell me how to keep our connection alive.

What I needed was someone to show me how to support us on a single income and still enjoy birthdays, Christmas, and date nights.

What I needed was someone to show me how to get through all the goddamn housework! And not to judge me for choosing to binge-watch Netflix rather than folding the laundry.

What I needed was someone to reassure me it was okay to be angry; to be sad; to want more out of life. Reassurance that I didn't have to give up on all my dreams.

I needed someone to tell me I didn't have to be perfect. I didn't have to be strong.

I needed to feel that there is no shame in our modest life held together by duct tape, nail polish, and love.

What I needed was someone to reassure me that I could do better than survive. I could learn to thrive. I could find meaning in all this crumpled laundry. What I needed was someone to show me how to squeeze joy out of this lemon of a life.

Chapter 3
What about me?

In my effort to cope with my situation, I sought out books and support groups. What resources I did find were written by professionals. They were helpful to learn about her illness. But it kept the focus on *her*. They didn't help me understand what was happening to *me*.

Unable to find what I needed, I wrote my own little guidebook. You're holding it in your hands.

This book is my message in a bottle. I am blowing it a light kiss and tossing it into the vast ocean of the galaxy. If you find it, I hope it is exactly what you need at this time in your life. This book is a love letter to you, to me, to us. It's a love letter to those who love someone who struggles to maintain a will to live in a world where mental illness is still regarded as a failure of character, where recovery is considered to be a simple matter of choice.

This book is meant for those of us who watch our loved ones hurt themselves; or make incomprehensible decisions; or live in a world out of sync with our own.

I want you to know that if you feel lost, helpless, alone and pissed as shit, you don't need to hide from everyone. You certainly don't need to hide from me.

I want to remind you that you are stronger than you feel. I know it is a cliche to say so, but it's true. A good portion of your energy is taken up by loving someone who can be hard to love sometimes. And yet, you do. That takes strength and empathy at black belt levels. And you persevere. Limping at times maybe, but you persevere.

And when things seem really desperate, when you're exhausted and wondering why, may this book remind you:

- That you're allowed to say no. In fact, you *should* say no. (Say it with me, one more time with feeling!)

- That you have limits and it's not admitting weakness to set them.

- That it's okay to focus on *you*. No matter what is happening with your loved one, it is not selfish to carve out joy and find beauty in the moment. There is power and restoration in meeting your own needs.

- That it takes energy to care for someone you love–in surprising ways sometimes. You are allowed to be tired and to rest.

- That you are allowed to be angry with the one you love. That doesn't mean your relationship is in trouble, or that someone is wrong. You must remember that sometimes it's not you or your loved one that is at fault. Sometimes, it's the illness in control. You didn't cause the illness, you can't control it and you can't fix it. You can only love each other *through* it.

- That you can feel two (or more) opposing feelings at the same time. It doesn't mean one is wrong and the other right. You don't have to choose one over the other. Feelings are never wrong. They just are. You can learn to embrace all of what you feel.

- That leaning into your feelings (even or especially when they're mixed) and taking responsibility for your issues and your mental health leads to profoundly satisfying relation-ships.

- That you don't have to be perfect. You don't have to keep up appearances.

- That just because you're grateful things aren't worse, doesn't mean they aren't fucking hard.

- That you are likely grieving. Scratch that. You *are* grieving. You are also experiencing caregiver stress or even burnout. If you aren't yet, you will.

- That in spite of it all, you have the right to enjoy life. You can still pick up a hobby. In fact, you must, because even when exhausted, spending energy on the right things *gives* you energy and healing.

- That help is available when you learn to ask for it. That allowing others to help is a gift you give to them, especially when it's your loved one and they struggle to help them-selves.

- That you must acknowledge how much you have on your plate.

- That you must remember what you love about the person you are caring for. You must nurture your relationship.

- That you can learn to plant your feet firmly in reality and still feel free. The key to that freedom is to stop hoping things will be different than they are. You can choose what you focus on and that will change your world.

- That leaning into your feelings (even or especially when they're mixed) and taking responsibility for your issues and your mental health leads to profoundly satisfying relationships.

- That even when exhausted, spending energy on the right things *gives* you energy.

When our Loved One struggles with their health, much of our focus goes towards their care: worrying for them, wishing better for them, brainstorming ways to contribute to their wellbeing. This fills our life with purpose and love.

But it also leaves little room for caring for ourselves. It skews our perspective on life and hijacks our energy. It's imperative that we remind ourselves who we are and claim our own space and time.

May this book help you do just that.

Chapter 4

How to use this book

This book is short. On purpose. You barely have time to read, let alone study. You can read this book in one sitting, or keep it by your bedside.

Hell, you can keep it in the bathroom and open it randomly to any chapter each time you go for a wizz. Each chapter is so short and to the point, you will be done by the time you're ready to wipe.

The title of each chapter is an affirmation or a promise: a reminder of your rights as a human being, or a promise you can make to your-self.

The meat of each chapter tackles a topic I myself have struggled with.

Following each topic are questions to help you explore the topic and how it relates to you and your circumstance. There is room after each chapter to journal, sketch, make lists, whatever strikes your fancy. Don't be precious. This book is yours. Use crayons, markers, fold the corners to keep your spot, or rip the pages out and carry them in your purse.

The book is cheap enough that if you want a clean copy, you can always buy another one.

Each chapter ends with a promise you will make to yourself. I leave room for you to fill in the blanks so that these promises are truly yours – your commitment to yourself.

Ready?

Let's begin...

Getting Real

Chapter 5

Being grateful things aren't worse doesn't mean they aren't fucking hard

Sometimes we think we don't have the right to feel the way we do because others "have it worse."

"What right do I have to complain?" we think. Which really means, "What right do I have to feel sad, or angry when there are people in the world who are homeless, or hungry, or grieving?"

This is a form of self-abandonment. We shame ourselves for struggling, so our feelings go unrecognized, unacknowledged and unshared. We suffer in silence, alone, which prolongs our suffering.

But both can be true. It can be true that we enjoy privilege in many areas of our lives, while at the same time we are struggling with the current situation.

Comparing suffering closes our hearts to the suffering of others.

The more we acknowledge and offer ourselves compassion for our own struggles, the more we will foster our capacity to have compassion for the struggles of others.

Journal Prompts:

What areas of my life am I struggling with?

Do I feel ashamed of my struggles when I compare them to others?

Affirmation:

This week I will show myself compassion by

____

Chapter 6

I can feel two (or more) opposing feelings at the same time

We can feel sad but also peaceful. We can feel disappointed but also hopeful. We can feel angry at the person we love most in the world.

Sometimes feeling two opposing feelings is confusing. It feels like they should cancel each other out. Or that one feeling must be a mistake.

The truth is, we are infinitely more complex as human beings than our minds can really grasp. Often we don't even know what exactly we are feeling. It may be clear to us that we are angry, but what's under the anger? Is it fear? Sadness? Disappointment?

We can feel a multitude of feelings at the same time – even feelings that seem contradictory. We even have words to describe contradictory feelings: words like bittersweet, nostalgia, or ambivalence.

The good news is, we don't really have to identify how we feel. We can embrace all the feelings without making sense of them. We can allow ourselves to feel everything we feel without judging ourselves for it. This is what it means to live life with our whole heart.

Journal Prompts:

What opposing feelings am I feeling that I am questioning?

What do I think it says about me to feel mixed feelings?

What would it feel like to give contradictory feelings room to be?

Affirmation:

This week, I will allow room for feeling all that I feel.

For example, right now I feel ____________________

I will remember that feelings are neither right nor wrong. They just are.

Chapter 7

I will face reality with loving kindness

Mental illness is unpredictable. There are days when our loved one wakes up cheerful and motivated. They radiate sunshine. On other days sadness is carved in the lines of their face. There is nothing we can do to change that. Nothing we can do to stem the tide of tears or extend the hours the sun shines. But still, we try. Oh, how we try!

Deep down we might believe that if we do the right things in the right order, somehow we can make it better. Maybe if we feed them the right foods. Maybe if they meditated more. Maybe if we made them walk more. Maybe if the doctors knew what the hell they were doing!

This tendency can go unchecked until it spills into all areas of our lives, until we are obsessively focused on the smallest details. Maybe we think that unless we have the right dish sponge we can't wash the dishes. Maybe we sweat over e-mails, making sure every single word conveys exactly what we mean to say, rewriting them over and over again. Maybe we get frustrated when others don't act as we think they should, and blame them for how things turn out.

It usually takes a very unpleasant consequence to shake us up, to remind us that we can't control as much as we unconsciously believe we can.

Yes, there are a lot of things in life that we do have control over. We can make things happen. We can put some order into our corner of the universe. But we *can't* bend reality to our will.

A LOT of what happens in life is unpredictable and uncontrollable. Death, taxes, and plagues come to mind. Much of life just *is*. The return to sanity is coming to terms with reality. There's no getting around it.

Reality for those of us who love someone with mental illness or who struggle with our own mental health is that life is often unpredictable and mostly uncontrollable.

Reality is that when our loved one is in pain, we hurt too. It means facing the fact that we are powerless to fix it. It means facing the fear that our future will have more pain, more struggle, and more grief.

Trying to avoid this future we are afraid of will make us sick. The more we try to control what our loved one does, eats or thinks, the closer we get to conflict. The more we try to avoid reality by what we eat, buy or do, the closer we are to losing our minds.

If we want to help our loved ones heal, if we want to create an environment where healing can happen and where we can live in some peace, we have to face our fears, our powerlessness, and our uncomfortable feelings. We have to come belly to belly with reality.

Journal Prompts:
What reality am I trying to avoid?

What is hardest for me to acknowledge about our situation and my powerlessness to do anything about it?

Affirmation:
This week, I will face the fact that ________________________________ and that ________________________________

I will give myself love and kindness as I face these facts.

Chapter 8

I will acknowledge how much I have on my plate

It's challenging to come home from a long day at work to find our loved one has barely moved. It is not their fault, we remind ourselves. We are able to work and that is a blessing. And so, we push through without acknowledging our difficult feelings.

We bury our sadness, our frustration, our disappointment, our grief, our loneliness. These feelings fester into resentment. Soon, we feel hopeless and depressed, without truly understanding why.

It's important to acknowledge that it can be challenging to carry a full load – a full-time job, a household to run – when our loved one is not.

We can share our burdens with a trusted friend. We can vent about our difficult day at work with our partner. The important thing is to allow ourselves to acknowledge the weight of our load and have another person validate those feelings.

When we feel heard, we can show up more fully for our loved one - without resentment.

Journal Prompts:

Make a list of all the responsibilities you carry:

Take a moment to acknowledge how much you have on your plate and how much strength and resilience it takes to manage.

Affirmation:

This week, I will acknowledge how much is on my plate. I will give myself credit for being strong, resilient and ___________________

Chapter 9

I will acknowledge that it takes energy to care for someone

Living requires physical, intellectual, and emotional energy. It is astounding how much energy it takes just to *be*. We believe we should be able to handle more than we actually can. We believe we should handle it all. We want to be *that* person: strong, brave, dependable, with a tidy kitchen.

It may seem like everyone else manages just fine, and still has the time and energy to reach their weight goals, train for a marathon, win pie contests, and start a side hustle.

We stare out the window numb and bone tired and wonder: *What the hell is wrong with me?*

There is nothing wrong with us.

Loving someone with mental health concerns takes energy in invisible ways. We worry about them, about the future. We feel sad that they are hurting. We feel disappointed at canceled plans, lack of income, unfulfilled potential. This too takes energy.

Here are some other invisible things that take energy:

- Watching someone you love struggle with their mental health;

- Holding space for someone you care about as they work through their healing;

- Holding space for your loved one to express their big feelings, especially when their feelings or the way they express them is triggering;

- Keeping your spirits up;

- Focusing on the positive;

- Getting bad news that you have no control over and can't change;

- Receiving a frightening diagnosis;

- Someone you love receiving a frightening diagnosis;

- Someone you love receiving an additional diagnosis when they are already struggling with a current disorder;

- Being disappointed when something you were hoping for fails to materialize;

- Having to change plans you were looking forward to;

- Living paycheck to paycheck;

- Realizing you can't afford something you were looking forward to, especially if that thing seemed reasonable;

- Spending time with people who can afford more than you can;

- Being unable to give your loved ones what you want to;

- Spending time with people who don't understand what you are going through;

- Spending time with people who don't understand what your loved one is going through;

- Living in a messy or cluttered environment;

- Cleaning or tidying up a space only to have it return to chaos a few hours later;

- Recognizing that your loved one is doing the best they can;

- Picking up the slack;

- Not having time to devote to what brings you joy;

- Not having the energy to devote to what brings you joy;

- Processing difficult feelings.

Journal Prompts:

What invisible thing is taking my energy that I am not recognizing?

Affirmation:

This week I will give myself the space and time to replenish my well

by _______________________

Chapter 10

I will acknowledge that I may be experiencing caregiver stress

Caregiver stress or burnout can creep up on us. It can be difficult to recognize. But it is nonetheless real. We may find it difficult to acknowledge unless it is diagnosed by a healthcare professional. But chances are, if we are caring for someone we love, we will at some point, if not already, experience caregiver stress or burnout.

Caregiver stress can manifest as sadness, frustration with ourselves or others, impatience with our loved one or others, We may experience despair and lose hope that things will ever improve. We may experience grief for the life we had planned for but is derailed by our loved one's illness. We may even blame our loved one for our circumstances, and then feel shame for having those thoughts.

It can even be difficult to give ourselves the compassion we need since we feel so depleted.

We may withdraw from family and friends. Lose interest in activities we used to enjoy. Feel blue, cranky, hopeless and helpless. We may experience changes in our appetite or weight, our sleep patterns. We may find we get sick more often, experience headaches, stomach pain or body pain.

We may feel emotionally or physically exhausted. We may use alcohol, drugs or medication too much. We may experience wanting to hurt ourselves or the person for whom we are caring. We may stay up late, withdraw from friends and family, or conversely become rigid and controlling.

All these feelings are natural. It is not an indication that we are failing at our role or our loved one. It is an indication that we are past our limits. It means it is time to ask for help.

We can ask for help by talking about our feelings to a trusted friend. We can speak with a therapist or join a support group. We can forge our own path by trying different things and sticking to what brings us relief.

Journal Prompts:

Which of the above symptoms am I experiencing?

Affirmation:

This week, I will notice if I am feeling any of the symptoms of caregiver stress or burnout. When I am, I will seek help by

Nurturing My Relationship

Chapter 11

I will remember what I love about the one I am caring for

When caregiver stress or burnout takes over our minds, it can be hard to remember who our loved one is beyond the illness. We spend so much time caring for their basic needs, we risk seeing them as a drain on our lives. This can creep up so insidiously, we may not even realize it's happening. We must make an effort to remember who they are and what we love about them.

We can keep a list of what we love most about them.

Sometimes the relationship suffers because it is hard to see past our caregiver role. Not only does this list remind us why we love them, it can also help rekindle the spark in the relationship.

This can also help our loved one remember that they are more than the illness they suffer. They are a full, worthy and valued human being, not merely a drain on our time and energy.

Mental illness is a challenge for romantic relationships. It can be alienating for us partners, leaving us feeling lonely and disconnected from the relationship. Eventually, the daily rituals and chores erode the sense of closeness and gratitude. It gets in the way of communication. It robs us of meaningful time together.

When we sacrifice ourselves and yet remain committed, we are no longer showing up as our full and true selves in the relationship.

We can make it a ground rule that our connection comes first. Our well-being depends on it. We can make nurturing our connection a priority.

Connection is like a fire, if we don't stoke it, it goes out.

We can plan to get together as soon as possible and reconnect as equals. We make time to get to know each other for the people we are today. We take stock and talk about what we appreciate about each other. Or we spend time doing something fun together.

It doesn't have to be elaborate or expensive. The HOW is less important than the intention to get reconnected.

We can go out to the local pub, without our phones, share an appetizer and talk. We can take a drive to somewhere we've never been. We can build a fort in our living room, eat junk food, and watch The Goonies. Whatever it is, the point is to really be with each other, get to know who we are now, and remember what it is we love about each other.

The quality of our connection is our safe space. It is what gives us the courage to keep showing up for life on life's terms.

Journal Prompts:

What qualities do I love most about the one I am caring for?

List their accomplishments or their good qualities. Read them to your loved one.

What is something you both enjoy doing together?

Affirmation:

This week, to reconnect with my loved one, I will___________________________________

Chapter 12

I will remember that I didn't cause it, I can't control it and I can't fix it

Those of us who care for loved ones sometimes fall into the trap of thinking we can control the illness. Because what we do is helpful to our loved one, because sometimes we do and say things that make them feel better, we begin to believe that we have control over the disorder. That in turn can lead us to believe that we can fix it, or at least make it better.

These are often unconscious beliefs. Our conscious minds know better! But deep down, some part of us can believe things that don't make sense to our conscious, logical minds. And these beliefs can influence our behavior.

When we become frustrated with our loved ones for not following our advice, we may be operating under the unconscious belief that we know better and can "fix" our loved one.

When they follow our advice but don't experience improvement, we may be operating under the unconscious belief that we are causing their distress.

When there is so much that we need to take care of, it's easy to fall into the belief that we are responsible. We end up trying to exert control over things that are not ours to control.

We might want to control their diet, for example. If only they would eat less junk food, we might think, and then refuse to buy it. We might follow it up by saying things like, "Are you sure you need more chips?" or "Didn't your doctor tell you you need to eat less salt?"

We might begin to nag them to go for walks. We might make snide comments about their weight.

Of course we are coming from a place of concern and care. We are worried they are hurting themselves. But when we are caregivers, it is easy to confuse caring with controlling.

Being controlling is an attempt to give ourselves relief from hard emotions and uncertainty. It is a sign that we need to care more intentionally for ourselves and our feelings rather than continue to focus on our loved one. We need to re-focus on ourselves.

Journal Prompts:

What about my loved one's condition is beyond my control?

1. ______________________________

2. ______________________________

3. ______________________________

What about my loved one's behavior is out of my control?

1. _______________________

2. _______________________

3. _______________________

If I surrendered control over

____,

how would that make me feel?

What does my loved one have the right to do that makes me uncomfortable or causes me worry?

Affirmation:

This week, I will be brave and surrender control over

____

If this causes me anxiety or other uncomfortable feelings, I will care for myself by _____________________________________

Chapter 13

I am allowed to be angry with my loved one

We are allowed to feel angry with someone we love. This does not mean we are wrong or bad. It could mean we are disappointed things aren't the way we imagined they would be. It could mean we are tired of carrying so much.

We may have judgments about being angry. We may feel we don't have the right to be angry at someone we love who is sick. What kind of person does that make us?

But anger is a feeling that we cannot avoid. It just means we are human.

Sometimes we may feel we need to act on our anger. This is natural. Anger is a motivating emotion. It spurs us into action. But not everything we are angry about requires us to take action.

That's when it's important to realize that just because something angers us doesn't mean someone is at fault. There isn't always someone to blame.

That is what makes anger so difficult to deal with. We know that lashing out at our loved one can damage the relationship. But what can we do when we feel this anger?

The first thing is to realize that being angry at our loved one doesn't mean we don't love them. It doesn't necessarily mean it's their fault (although it could be). It just means we are feeling frustration or disappointment. Sometimes we just need to feel and express it safely to someone we trust, and who cares for us. Expressing it in a safe context can make us feel better, more present to ourselves and to our relationships.

Journal Prompts:
What am I angry about but afraid to say?
What am I angry about but don't feel I have the right to be?

Affirmation:
This week, I will give myself a little space to feel my anger. I will express it safely by ________________

I will remember that being angry at my loved one, doesn't mean I don't love them.

Letting the Outside World In

Chapter 14

I don't have to keep up appearances

None of us want to stand out for the wrong reasons. We want to be the same or better than our neighbors and friends. An untidy home, a weedy garden, a hastily bought or cheap birthday gift can make us feel like we are not measuring up. We are not keeping up with everyone else. We are not living up to our responsibilities as a functioning adult. And this brings up shame.

For generations, people have carried shame about having a sick relative at home to care for – especially if the sickness was mental illness.

We avoid acknowledging it. We work twice as hard to keep up the appearance of coping – managing to care for our loved one as well as our household, our other family members, our work, our garden, our commitments.

We think that not managing is a sign of weakness. We may think others are pitying us, which makes us feel inferior to others in our own eyes and in the eyes of others.

But we really don't have to keep up appearances. Our circumstances are what they are. We can show courage by standing tall and accepting them. A well kept garden, an impeccable home, an expensive birthday present – these are not a measure of who we are, or our value as human beings.

Who we are is someone who prioritizes caring for someone we love.

Who we are is someone who loves deeply.

Who we are is someone who prioritizes spending time with our loved one over housework.

At the end of life, no one regrets spending more time folding laundry, or buying a more expensive birthday gift. One regrets not spending more time with loved ones.

We are ahead of the curve.

Journal Prompts:

Do I feel the need to keep up appearances?

How did I learn this?

What do my actions show about my priorities?

Affirmation:

When I feel shame about not keeping up appearances, I will remind myself that I am prioritizing ________________________

Chapter 15

I will choose my friends wisely

We are great friends to others. We are caring, considerate and thoughtful. We can handle big emotions when tragedies strike. We have containers of frozen lasagna and soup in our freezers when these are required by friends. We have a great sense of humor for absurd situations.

And then there are times when we seem to disappear to our friends. Times when we have to cancel plans at the last minute. Times when we forget birthdays or anniversaries. There can be days, even weeks without contact.

We go through phases when we are in survival mode, when caring for ourselves and our loved one is about all we can manage. With much of your energy directed homeward, we have little energy to spare.

During these times, we can feel lonely and disconnected. So we withdraw. Instead of risking disappointing our friends, we pull away. Instead of feeling shame over forgetting an important event in a friend's life, we let the friendship lapse.

Our best friends are low maintenance friends. They are people who allow us to be thoroughly vulnerable. People who can laugh with us at the awkward absurdity of it all. People who can put up with our loved one when medication takes away their social filters. People who can handle a good cry.

We need people who put up with last minute cancellations, and don't get offended when we forget their birthday.

Let's face it: we are a mixed bag. And that's ok. It's ok to be a mixed bag. It's ok to have good stretches and not so good stretches. It doesn't mean we are bad friends, or that we can't contribute in a meaningful way to a fulfilling friendship.

Journal Prompts:

How would I describe my relationship with my friends?
Are there ways in which I feel I am not a good friend?
Do I have friends who understand the pressures I am under?

Affirmation:

This week, I will connect with ___________________.
I will tell them I appreciate that they show up for me in the following ways _________________________________.

Chapter 16

I will be completely honest with two or three friends

Suffering in silence is the greatest threat to our mental and physical health. We need to be able to feel and express the whole range of emotions in order to maintain our wellbeing.

A number of studies confirm that suppressing or bottling up our emotions can impact our blood pressure, memory and self-esteem. Avoiding emotions can lead to anxiety and depression.

Emotional stress can actually shorten our lifespan. Bottling up our feelings literally threatens our lives.

Eventually, the constant stress will lead to outbursts of anger or tears. We might be angry at our spouse and bottle up the emotion. Then later in the day, we lash out at a coworker. That explosion and overreaction is our body's way of releasing that pent-up emotion.

We must find ways to talk about our feelings without fear of judgment. We must be able to vent out the frustration or sadness or grief.

This doesn't mean we have to tell everyone we encounter our deepest, most uncomfortable feelings. But it does mean we have to become vulnerable and find ways to express them safely. Support groups are great for this purpose since everyone in the group can relate and identify with what we are going through.

We can enlist two or three friends who understand and appreciate our circumstances, are good listeners and are able to keep what we share in confidence. We can commit to sharing our feelings with them. All our feelings. Especially the ones we feel shame around.

Doing so helps us feel connected to humanity. It helps us feel less alone. By opening up, we encourage others to do the same. It makes us feel good to be there for them also, when they struggle.

Journal Prompts:

Do I bottle up my uncomfortable emotions?

What feelings do I find the hardest to express?

Who can I be honest with without fear of judgment?

Do I have a friend I can tell anything to?

How does that make me feel?

Affirmation:

This week, I will confide in________________

I will be available for my friend to share their most challenging feelings also.

If I don't have a friend to confide in, I will

________________ to ensure that I don't keep my feelings bottled up.

Chapter 17

I will let others help me

It's astounding how often help is available when we dare to ask for it. There is often shame associated with needing help, like we don't have our shit together. So we don't ask for help. We prefer to suffer alone rather than to feel the pain of being judged for our inability to cope.

We may feel overwhelmed, but are afraid to impose on others. We don't want to be a burden. After all, we know what it feels like to have a lot on our plate. So even when people ask what they can do to support us, we tell them we are fine.

When we say "Thanks but I don't need anything really, I'm fine," We are closing the door on someone who is asking how they could show us they care.

Or maybe we want to ask for help but don't know what to ask for.

But people are more creative and generous than we give them credit for. We can let them make suggestions.

Start by finding something that isn't difficult to do and that will genuinely help. It could be sending us funny memes to brighten up our day. It could be getting a quart of milk next time they go to the grocery store. It could be picking us up for a walk.

Journal Prompts:

Do I find it challenging to ask for help?

What beliefs do I have about asking for help?

What can I say next time someone asks how they can support me?

Affirmation:

This week, when someone asks me if they can help, I will let them. I will let someone show me that they care.

Caring For Self

Chapter 18

I am allowed to have limits

Having limits does not mean we are flawed. It does not mean we are incapable. Everything has limits. Everything has an expiration date. Everyone falters when pushed too hard – even Olympic athletes.

Those of us who care for loved ones – who don't think twice when a loved one requires help – don't always recognize our limits. We wonder why we are tired. We wonder why we fail to show up after having shown up consistently for the last 23 months; why we forget things; why we snap; why we feel listless; why we feel hopeless. What is wrong with us?

It seems inconceivable that we should have limits, let alone reach them. After all, caring for loved ones is rewarding. It generates its own energy. We feel energized and reassured when our loved one is tucked in safely, their bellies full, their needs met. And this masks our own fatigue. This makes it hard to recognize when we have reached our own limits, when we are depleted.

We use the comfort and reassurance of caring for our loved one as a way to fill our well. But our well can run dry. If we don't take time to replenish, we will no longer feel rewarded by taking care of our loved one. We will begin to resent them. This is called caregiver fatigue, or caregiver stress, or compassion fatigue.

Journal Prompts:

Who am I when I am depleted?

How does that feel?

How will I know when I am reaching my limits?

What will I do to replenish my well?

Affirmation:

This week, I will recognize that I have limits. I will stop

____

when I feel _________

And instead, I will _________________

Chapter 19

I am allowed to be tired and to rest

Needing rest does not mean we are failing our loved one.

Caring for another as well as one's self demands energy. We all need time to rest. That might look like an afternoon nap; or curling up on the couch with tea and a good book; or simply staring into the distance.

For many of us, resting or taking time to "do nothing" can be a challenge, especially if there is a mountain of laundry waiting to be washed, or dishes to be cleaned, or a loved one struggling with their mental health issues. .

We berate ourselves for being "lazy." We bully ourselves into getting up and working. We tell ourselves that we will feel better after the house is clean, after the week's dinners and lunches are made, after the laundry is finally folded.

At other times, we can't bring ourselves to do anything. Instead, we lie on the couch scrolling through social media. Or we watch TV. Or stare into space. Or fall asleep.

These are sure signs that we have reached caregiver fatigue. Yet we feel as though we are failing our loved one. After all, we are capable. We are well. We should be on top of things.

We need to remind ourselves that even able, capable, and healthy human beings need rest. Rest is a need, not a reward for good behavior, or reserved only for those who are ill.

Journal Prompts:

How do I feel about needing rest?

Do I recognize when I need rest?

What kind of rest do I need? (Physical, emotional, mental, social, creative, or spiritual?)

Affirmation:

This week, I will acknowledge that I need rest when I feel

____

When I feel that feeling, I know I need (physical, mental, emotional, spiritual) _______________________________________ rest.

I will _______________________________

Chapter 20
I will say "no" more often

Those of us who care for others often find it challenging to say *no*. Saying *no* may make us feel guilty. We may even feel shame, as though we are being selfish, or callous, or rude. We may feel that whatever we are capable of doing, we should do.

Our inability to say *no* can cost us. In fact, when our bodies, minds and souls are begging us to say *"no,"* saying *"yes"* can hurt us.

Sometimes we don't even recognize when we should say *no*. When saying *no* feels bad, we are more likely to say *yes*, even when we need to pause, rest, and nurture our spirits.

Yes, of course we will help. Yes, of course we will go to that birthday party on the weekend. Yes, of course we will give up our free time. After all, we are "doing nothing" during this free time. Who are we to say *no*?

Are we really allowed to say *no*?

Yes, we are! In fact, we need to say *no* more often. We need time to pause and reflect. We need time to recharge.

If it feels rude to say *no* to others, remember that there are many ways to say *no* that are gentle, friendly, and kind. For example, we might say:

"Is it urgent? Can it wait until later?"

"Not at this time, but thank you for thinking of me."

"I have another commitment, but I hope you'll invite me again." (Commitments to ourselves count!)

"That sounds wonderful, maybe some other time?"

Remind yourself that you are allowed to say *no*. You don't have to say *no* all the time, or every time, or forever. Just practice it now and again. Start small. See what happens...

Journal Prompts:

What prompts me to say "yes" when I really want to say *no*?

How does saying *no* make me feel?

How does saying yes make me feel?

Affirmation:

This week, I will say no to (person or request)

____

If asked, my response will be ____________________

Chapter 21

I don't have to be perfect.

Perfection is a made up concept we have been developing since we were children. From a very early age, we were taught to "measure up" to our siblings and our peers. We learned that when we got close to other people's expectations – our parents, our teachers – they were happy with us. The sun shone brighter in our sky, and it made us feel safe. It made us feel valued.

The farther we got from their expectations – when we disappointed our parents or teachers – clouds gathered. We felt threatened, burdened.

We may have been told explicitly what it was to be perfect: a far distant land we could never quite reach. Or we may not have been told what it was to be perfect. It may have felt like we were playing a game of blindfolded soccer with moving goalposts.

The echoes of this childhood contest still lives within us. We've internalized the yard stick. In the process we have become our own harshest critic. This drive to be close to perfect keeps us feeling like we are never good enough. We are always failing. Or perhaps we get close, we feel the sun on our faces. But when we awake the next day, there are clouds in our skies. What will it take today to be "perfect"?

Perfection doesn't really exist. It's a made-up concept. That's good news, because it means we get to define "perfect" for ourselves. We get to choose what is good enough for us today.

Journal Prompts:

What do I believe perfect looks like?

What is good enough for me today?

Affirmation:

This week, I will remember that "perfect" is a made-up concept.

When   I   feel   bullied   by   perfectionism,   I   will

____

Chapter 22

I have the right to enjoy life even when my loved one is depressed

I t can be hard to feel good when our loved one is not.

When we feel joy but our loved one feels depressed, we can experience terrible guilt. Maybe we're afraid our joy might be offensive to them, or might make things worse, like pouring salt in a wound. So we temper our behavior, acting more subdued than we feel, downplaying our happiness, and accentuating the negatives.

"Things are ok," we might say, "not great."

Maybe we become frustrated with our loved one's dark mood. We try pushing, sulking, nagging, pleading. We try to change how they feel, or convince them that they don't feel as bad as all that. After all, the sun is shining! We can't spend our lives in the dark. Often we find ourselves walking on eggshells because we don't want our loved one to feel anything big, because it adds to the burden of responsibility that we may already feel.

This is the perfect breeding ground for resentment.

Eventually, we may deny ourselves because enjoying ourselves can feel disloyal. Taking care of our souls and being delighted feels like betrayal. So we wallow, waiting for them to return so that we too can enjoy things again.

If we do go out and enjoy ourselves, we can feel especially lonely. We don't want to be experiencing these things by ourselves. We want them with us, enjoying with us, delighting with us, laughing with us, discovering with us.

So it seems right to stay home, to curl up next to them and wait for the sun to reappear instead of dancing in the rain.

But as counter-intuitive as it appears, we must put on our rain boots, kiss them gently on the forehead and head out. It is not betrayal to carve out joy where we can find it. It is not being disloyal to enjoy ourselves. It is refilling our tank. It is going out to collect moments of joy and returning to our loved one with a bouquet of sunshine to light their way home.

Journal Prompts:

Do I feel guilty for enjoying moments of pleasure when my loved one is struggling?

What will I do this week that is just for me?

How will I invite more joy into my life?

Affirmation:

This week, I will allow myself to feel joy when it bubbles up. When I start to feel guilty, I will _______________________

Chapter 23
I will pick up a hobby

We may not remember a time when we did something frivolous just for ourselves. Played with paints just to watch the colours blend, or wrote stories without worrying if they were good enough to publish. Maybe it seemed like a waste of time, or maybe it seemed like too much work, or too much energy was required or it was too expensive.

Here's a secret: spending energy on a hobby actually gives us more energy.

It's one of those bits of ordinary life magic: If we take time out to do something we enjoy, instead of feeling depleted, we feel refreshed.

We can start with something simple and cheap: dollar store paints, flour and water, a crochet hook and some yarn, maybe some Youtube videos.

Remember, it's about claiming time to feed our spirits. We stake a claim in the river of time. It is ours to waste as we see fit. Challenge the slave driver in our head and flip it the bird. We can be a rebel and steal time, then waste it.

We can reclaim the neglected parts of ourselves and feel whole again.

Journal Prompts:

Finish this sentence:

I've always wanted to_________________

Or I wonder if I could_______________

What step will I take tomorrow to begin my journey?

Affirmation:

This week, I will ___________________, for <dura-tion>_________________.

Chapter 24

I will create a plan of care for myself

When our loved one struggles with their health, much of our focus goes towards their care, towards worrying for them, wishing better for them, and brainstorming ways to contribute to their wellbeing. This fills our life with purpose and love.

But when this focus is interrupted – such as when our loved one is hospitalized or goes into treatment -- it can leave us feeling lost and aimless. When the daily pressure is off, it might be a good time to turn the focus back on ourselves.

But we don't have to wait for our loved one to be hospitalized. Creating a plan of care for ourselves can help us regain some sense of control.

Use the template below to get you started.

My Plan of Care:

Three things I will ask for help with:

    1. ________________________

2. ___________________________

3. ___________________________

Three things I will do to take care of myself emotionally:

1. ___________________________

2. ___________________________

3. ___________________________

Three things I will do to take care of myself physically:

1. ___________________________

2. ___________________________

3. ___________________________

Three things I will do to take care of myself mentally:

1. ___________________________

2. ___________________________

3. ___________________________

Three things I will do to take care of myself financially:

1. ___________________________

2. ___________________________

3. ___________________________

Three things I will do to take care of myself socially:

1. ___________________________

2. ___________________________

    3. ______________________

Who are my supportive friends?

I will reach out to _________________ when I feel

____

Reminders for when I feel sad or discouraged:

____

____

Chapter 25
References

I did a little research for this book.

Wolff, J. L., Mulcahy, J. J., Huang, J., Roth, D., Covinsky, K. E., & Kasper, J. D. (2018, November 3). *Family Caregivers of Older Adults, 1999–2015: Trends in Characteristics, Circumstances, and Role-Related Appraisal*. Gerontologist; Oxford University Press. https://doi.org/10.1093/geront/gnx093

Mental Health of Caregivers. (2011, January 1). https://www.apa.org. https://www.apa.org/pi/about/publications/caregivers/practice-settings/assessment/tools/mental-health-caregivers

Rospenda, K. M., Minich, L., Milner, L. A., & Richman, J. A. (2010, July 14). *Caregiver Burden and Alcohol Use in a Community Sample*. Journal of Addictive Diseases; Taylor & Francis. https://doi.org/10.1080/10550887.2010.489450

WebMD Editorial Contributors. (2020, January 19). *Compassion Fatigue: Symptoms to Look For*. WebMD. https://www.webmd.com/mental-health/signs-compassion-fatigue

Heyl, J. C. (2022, February 15). *After Two Years of COVID, Are We Running Out of Empathy?* Verywell Mind. https://www.verywellmind.com/are-we-running-out-of-empathy-5215836

Caregiver stress: Tips for taking care of yourself. (2022, March 22). Mayo Clinic. https://www.mayoclinic.org/healthy-lifestyle/stress-management/in-depth/caregiver-stress/art-20044784

Luethi, M., Meier, B. H., & Sandi, C. (2008, January 1). *Stress effects on working memory, explicit memory, and implicit memory for neutral and emotional stimuli in healthy men.* Frontiers in Behavioral Neuroscience; Frontiers Media. https://doi.org/10.3389/neuro.08.005.2008

Galanakis, M., Palaiologou, A., Patsi, G., Velegraki, I., & Darviri, C. (2016, May 12). *A Literature Review on the Connection between Stress and Self-Esteem.* Psychology; Scientific Research Publishing. https://doi.org/10.4236/psych.2016.75071

Gross, J. J., & Muñoz, R. F. (1995, June 1). *Emotion regulation and mental health.* Clinical Psychology-science and Practice; Wiley-Blackwell. https://doi.org/10.1111/j.1468-2850.1995.tb00036.x

Chapman, B. P., Fiscella, K., Kawachi, I., Duberstein, P. R., & Muennig, P. A. (2013, October 1). *Emotion suppression and mortality risk over a 12-year follow-up.* Journal of Psychosomatic Research; Elsevier BV. https://doi.org/10.1016/j.jpsychores.2013.07.014

Can always staying positive be bad for our health? | HCF. (n.d.). https://www.hcf.com.au/health-agenda/body-mind/mental-health/downsides-to-always-being-positive

About the Author

Ran Weingartner, The Hospitable Alien, was dropped onto Earth shortly after the moon landing. Believing it to be more than mere chance, she tirelessly seeks a way back "home" while embracing her role as a dedicated steward of her adopted planet. Surviving addiction and trauma, Ran extracts profound meaning from life's hardships, sharing her insights with fellow travelers in an effort to heal and connect. Nestled in Northern Ontario, Canada, she writes alongside her wife Molly and loyal canine companion, Charlie. Join The Hospitable Alien on a transformative journey, as her words ignite the imagination and unlock the power of empathy.

You can find more of her writings here:
Website/ blog: www.HospitableAlien.com
Instagram: @hospitablealien
Facebook: The Hospitable Alien
Twitter: @RansFutureTrip

www.ingramcontent.com/pod-product-compliance
Lightning Source LLC
Chambersburg PA
CBHW021342160726
47994CB00007B/2821